RYA

# SIX FIGURE SALES RECRUITER

**BY**

**RYAN HOHMAN**

YouTube: Ryan Hohman SRU

Facebook: RyanHohmanSRU

Instagram: ryanhohman_sru

LinkedIn: Ryan Hohman

Ordering Information: Quantity sales. Special discounts are available on quantity purchases by corporations, associations, and others. Orders by U.S. trade bookstores and wholesalers.

www.DreamStartersPublishing.com

# Table of Contents

# Dedication

---

Before we dive into Six Figure Sales Recruiter and put you on a path to start accomplishing every single one of your sales recruiting goals, I'd like to thank God, my foundation in everything I do. I'm so grateful to have the opportunity to be an entrepreneur in this beautiful country we call, The USA, and my life is His.

I'd also like to thank my beautiful wife Monica; she has been instrumental in helping me build our recruiting business, and I wouldn't be able to do any of this without her. It's because of her help that I'm able to do things that I love, like write this book for all of you. I love you, Angel.

*"Husbands, love your wives, as Christ loved the church and gave himself up for her."*

**Ephesians 5:25**

*salesrecruitingu.com*

# Foreword

By Sales Rabbit VP, Zac Kerr

---

Your problem is that you are incredibly talented at your business - whatever product or service you sell, you do it well. But what you don't do well is; attracting, recruiting, hiring, firing, on-boarding, training, retaining, and promoting your single greatest asset: your people. You are normal. I have stared into the operating guts of thousands of companies just like yours and the majority haven't figured it out. So, what's to figure out!?

I've learned that the clients who win at solving their people problems also become scaleable sales orgs who thrive. These are the ones who live by this untold secret: They see themselves as a recruiting company first, sales company second, and fulfillment company 3rd. This simple paradigm shift is foundational.

I met Ryan when I hired him to architect a multi-state recruiting campaign for our rooftop solar business. We were already successful as the 5th largest solar originator in the nation. We were already a recruiting first, sales second, mentality organization. But as we grew various channels, we needed someone solely focused on filling the pipeline with prospective hires for our localized sales managers to interview and vet out. Ryan built us a great process, but over the last few years he's optimized and radically elevated his entire approach. As someone who has hired and on-boarded over 2500 Sales Reps in my career, I've learned that recruiting is the lifeblood to a thriving sales organization. In my current role, I observe a tremendous amount of various sales organizations selling a variety of services, in a variety of countries, the pattern is clear: those who see themselves as a recruiting company first, builds systems, processes, training, culture and leaders who honor this foundational practice of people attraction and cultivation. I urge every individual across the organization to become a master at recruiting.

"But It's hard." It's also hard to make Grannies family secret Mole sauce. Unless you have the recipe and someone who can exemplify how it's done. Someone who has been a student of the recipe and studied it again and again and again, with a lot of different variables in play. Ryan's content is super focused on the outcome of his learnings and because he's a student of the art and science of mastering the special sauce of recruiting, I see him as uniquely qualified to guide you through building your best organization yet.

I'm constantly asked, "can you refer me to a company that can do my recruiting or selling for me?" And therein is the opportunity for you. All of your competitors are wanting to remain as a fulfillment business. They aren't wanting to become the recruiting arm itself. They don't want to study the art and science of people systems. And as a result, they will always be subject to their organic growth. Ryan has created a unique hybrid offering to help you master the attributes of a recruiting first, sales second organization, while offering services that help fill the funnel to building your own sales organization. What I love most about building your own sales organization is that it gives you a tremendous platform to create demand for whatever product or service you are selling. I've seen the lives of business owners dramatically change based on the state of health in their recruiting and sales organization. There is a tremendous amount of energy available to you as an entrepreneur as you focus on the state and health of your sales organization.

Sales people require interaction and we tend to think it's going to take a lot of our energy. I made the mistake of thinking that those interactions drained me. I've realized, interactions sustain me. Interactions between a servant-based leader and his team creates energy. When a sales team is humming, there are few departments I want to be around more. I love the energy of healthy recruiting and sales orgs. It's been said "sales is the steam engine of the economy."

But none of it happens unless you shift to becoming a "recruiting first, sales second" organization. Doing this requires understanding what ingredients go into This Special Sauce. What kinds of behaviors, culture, processes, systems, events, commitments, technology is involved to create a sustainable steady drop of new recruits?

Let's read on to find out, I'm a continual student always curious to learn, so I'm grateful to read Ryan's work on this important topic.

**Zac Kerr - Sales Rabbit**
Partner, VP of Business Development

# Chapter 1

# You Need Proven Systems To Recruit Top Performers

---

Throughout this book, I want to bring to light the fact that you can accomplish what you want to accomplish, building an incredible sales team and leveraging that team to reach levels in your career that you've only dreamt of up until this point. Sales recruiting is tough; maybe one of the most difficult aspects of the sales industry, but YOU can become great at it. That's my guarantee. Most sales managers, entrepreneurs and owners put themselves in a place where recruiting gets neglected because it's difficult, and unfortunately this puts them in a massive disadvantage. Without a core commitment to the recruitment of a reliable, high producing sales team, no sales organization can get to where they want to be.

I've realized lately that one of my responsibilities as an entrepreneur who has mastered the systems and processes around the topic of recruiting, is to empower other entrepreneurs like you with the tools necessary to accomplish exactly what I have. Ultimately, if you want to build a REAL organization that doesn't require you to wear 20 hats every single day, then you need proven systems and operational processes for every aspect of your business. The steps and ideas that I outline in this book will help you outline those systems and processes necessary to build an incredible sales team, so that you can step out of wearing those 20 hats and work ON your business versus working IN your business. If you're an entrepreneur, the last thing I want for you is to be your own top sales person for the next 10 years. You deserve more than that, and you deserve an organization that is firing at all cylinders. A sales organization that allows you to step out of the sales role, and ideally even the sales management role, so that you can build a REAL business that you love running. Every. Single. Day.

Sales driven companies tend to stay stagnant or sometimes even fail whenever the owner-entrepreneur (Sometimes the sales manager as well depending on the situation) is the lead sales person; when everything lives and dies by their personal production. But once the owner-entrepreneur let's go of that responsibility and starts delegating sales to a capable team, they see their business skyrocket. And now, that owner-entrepreneur can be a true business person - working on their business versus working in their business. If this sounds like you, and if delegating the sales to a top performing team never happens down the road, then you will always be in some type of a rat race, probably not loving what you're doing long term, putting you in a place where you can never truly get ahead to realize the full potential of your organization. If this doesn't sound like you, and if you already have leadership in place with an incredible sales program, then congrats. You have an even easier path ahead of you, just keep reading.

See, I often meet well-intentioned entrepreneurs who handle the recruitment aspect of their business on their own, which is completely fine in certain circumstances when done correctly. But what typically happens is they'll hire two, three or four sales reps, and those individuals don't pan out, or even if one does, he or she puts in a sale or two then drops off. So, the owner "gives up," and starts thinking that "people just don't want to work hard anymore," or that there "isn't any talent in this area like other markets," or even that "people just don't want to work on commission anymore." But the truth is that the problem doesn't reside in the poor recruits they've brought on in the past, or in the fact that the company can't offer a salary, or that people just don't work hard anymore (whatever the excuse is). The REAL problem is that only 5% of sales organizations on this planet actually know how to recruit well, and they're simply not a part of that group yet. They're a part of the 95% trying to recruit, here and there, but consistently failing in scaling up their sales team and production, taking no responsibility for their lack of success in this area of their business. The 95% simply just have it wrong, and making it right first starts with transitioning the "mindset" to understanding that they can actually accomplish their goals. They need to transition their mindset and run their organization in a way that aligns with what Zac Kerr from Sales Rabbit said, "The best sales organizations in the world see themselves as a recruiting company first, sales company second, and fulfillment company third."

But recruiting is beyond getting someone to just sign on the dotted line and agree to work as a sales representative. As important, if not even more important, is the practice of recruiting the right people and providing an incredible onboarding and training experience for them, followed up by a top notch culture. In this book, I'll be guiding you to implement proven systems, processes and strategies around these topics so that you can build the sales team that you've always dreamt of.

When I first got into recruiting as an entrepreneur at 24, I didn't realize that recruiting sales reps and qualified leadership was actually the most difficult thing companies were facing when trying to grow their sales organization. I just thought that recruiting was going to be a quick path to income and entrepreneurial success.

I actually fell into this idea because of my buddy Myles. We were hanging out and talking about starting businesses, and the difficulties that come along with doing that. At the same time, he was managing job boards, messaging people online, and adding their names to some list. I asked him, "Myles, what are you doing?" He glanced up at me and said, "I'm scheduling interviews for Hodari." Hodari was the sales manager at my first sales job a few years back. Myles and I worked there together in Orange County, CA selling SEO marketing services for a couple years. I was intrigued with what Myles was doing so I kept asking him questions, and after about 10 minutes of digging in and getting a brief glimpse of what he was helping Hodari with, I knew that there was something of value there, potentially a business idea that could turn into something super cool. So, I dug in even more, and within a very short period of time (because I'm a pretty impulse kind of dude) I was convinced that this was "my winner," and probably my last chance at starting a potentially successful business before having to go back into full-time mortgage sales, which was my second sales job.

Since my three failed entrepreneurial attempts, I was struggling cash-wise. In fact, I was almost out of money, so I had to figure out something fast before having to go back to the corporate life again which was something I dreaded. I went from making 10 to 20 grand per month as a mortgage sales rep with a bunch of cash in the bank to a broke entrepreneur in under six months. I felt stupid at the time for leaving such a high-income job to become a broke entrepreneur, but I stuck it out.

During that six month period I made some pretty poor investments and even sold my truck that I loved to eliminate some of my monthly expenses. I was doing everything in my power to prevent myself from having to go back to the corporate world. I had less than $1,500 to my name so I had to figure things out fast. If I didn't come up with some cash within 2-3 weeks, I would've been asking for money from friends and family. That would've been super embarrassing because everyone thought I was uber successful after hearing about the money I was making in mortgage.

But this whole recruiting thing seemed to make sense to me, and I could see myself selling the service even though I had no idea what I was doing at the time. I actually look back, as a somewhat successful business owner today and crack up at the fact that I jumped into something I knew nothing about. It's probably not something I would do today, but God allowed things to work out.

Long story short, I jumped right into sales recruiting as a service. My buddy Myles was there to help me get down the basics, he showed me the ropes on what he was doing and in a fairly short period of time I was able to put together a sales recruiting business that, after five years now, has become highly successful, serving many high-end sales organizations all over the country that hire high-volumes of commission-based sales reps.

But besides the help from Myles, there was really nothing out there to help me become better at recruiting. It was all a trial-by-fire type of learning, and like today, information about sales recruiting was virtually non-existent. This surprised me, for what seemed to be such a vital component of business success; you couldn't just jump online and find tons on the topic like you could for sales. So, although looking back and realizing it was a good thing that I was forced to learn everything I know today, it also sucked because I was basically on my own in figuring this stuff out.

That first year of running my company was a roller-coaster. I was building the business, landing clients, and working like crazy to try and figure out some type of system to scale a low-cost recruiting service. Although recruiting sounded simple in nature, I realized over time that doing it right (Having the end-result of actual sales production from the new recruits) was actually very difficult. I realized over time that it's only simple once a proven system and process is fully in place, pumping out predictable recruiting and sales production results. It was hard to get to that point. The strategies that I'll be outlining in this book have taken me

YEARS to put together and it's turned out to be crazy valuable to sales organizations all across the country.

I knew nothing when I started recruiting in 2013, but what I did have was the confidence that if I worked hard enough, that I would become the best high volume, commission-based sales recruiter in the world, and that I'd end up building an incredible career by leveraging that skill set to work with people just like you. I went all in, laser-focused, and stuck it out. At first, when I was just getting started, surprisingly, clients loved what I was doing for them. I realized later that they loved my services because they were simply clueless about recruiting and didn't even know where to start. Most of them winged everything.

Their feedback gave me the confidence to continue to work through the pain of entrepreneurship and everything that comes along with creating a business. The goal has always been to be the best in the world at the systems and processes involved with high volume, commission-based sales recruiting.

In my mind, I'll probably never be the best in the world because my goals are always way beyond where I'm currently at, but I know with 100% certainty that I can impact your organization in a way that nobody else on this planet can, even if you fall into that top 5% who actually knows what they are doing. You may be a part of the 95% of organizations that do not know how to recruit, and in a sense, that's OK because most are in that same boat, but it is not OK if you actually want to grow a top performing sales team.

Here's what I've realized with absolute certainty, organizations don't suck at recruiting because they're not talented or have a crappy opportunity; it's simply because they haven't gone through enough sessions at the school of hard knocks to understand the systems and processes involved in effective recruitment.

With my guidance, and a little trial and error, you'll be able to build your dream sales organization, effectively and predictably. You will soon recognize that recruiting and retaining a high-quality sales team is the make or break aspect of being a successful sales company, and that it can't be ignored or relegated to a second-class priority. But it takes massive action.

Doing anything less is crazy! Why would you not make the most important part of building your company the number one priority? Some organizations aren't recruiting simply because they hate it and would rather stay where they are today so they don't have to deal with the time and financial investment that goes into building a rockstar team. But why?

I get it. It's hard work, it can be expensive, and dealing with new sales reps can be a pain, but building a great company will always be hard, for everyone. You're either in the top 5% of companies that know how to recruit and you're blowing up and accomplishing what you know is possible, or you're completely lost and frustrated and a part of the 95% that have no idea what they're doing.

Excuses never help. A struggling business can't continue to blame it on, "how things have changed" or that, "people just don't work hard anymore" or that, "I can't find any good sales people" or that, "people just don't like working on commission." The list goes on and on. Just cut the crap, step up and be a freaking REAL entrepreneur. The hustle is real, and the hustle can hurt if you want to create the dream life.

So, let me wrap this first chapter up by asking you a couple of questions. Would you like to join the 5% of sales organizations on this planet that are great at recruiting? And would you like to look at recruiting and onboarding as an exciting thing to do, versus it just being a pain in your neck? Yep, we both know your answer. And that's good, because this book was written so that you can short-cut your success to effective recruiting, and not have to go through the pain that I did over several years to figure this stuff out.

It's clear that when studying extremely successful people that they all have very similar advice, and one of those very well-known pieces of advice around the topic of learning from others, is by noted author and motivational speaker, the late, great Jim Rohn. He said, "It's important to learn from your mistakes, but it is BETTER to learn from other people's mistakes, and it's BEST to learn from other people's successes. It accelerates your own success."

That makes sense, right? Yep. It does. And let me tell you, I have FAILED over and over again at this recruiting thing, but over time, I've become a master at it. And it's time for me to take my recruiting successes and transfer those successes, systems, processes and strategies to you. That's what this book is all about. It's about you having the right information to actually execute on building your dream sales team, so that you can move closer to the vision you have for your career in this beautiful industry we call sales.

So commit, stay laser focused, and get through the whole book. Implement the tips included here, and watch your business grow! If you're not growing, you're dying. If you're not recruiting, all the time, you're not growing, and therefore you are dying. So let's dive in.

## Hohman's Homework

Where do you want your monthly sales production/revenue to be? Why do you want it to be there? Make sure you have a GREAT enough reason for WHY you want to accomplish these goals, or you will never work hard enough to get there.

What is the monthly average sales production/revenue per rep at your company? Or what should it be? From there, how many reps do you need to be hitting your monthly sales production/revenue goals?

When do you want to accomplish these goals by? By what time do you want to accomplish these goals? Be realistic.

What do you feel needs to change to accomplish these goals? It could be as simple as actually making recruiting a priority, or putting a budget aside to invest into recruiting etc.

______________________________________________

______________________________________________

______________________________________________

If you do not learn how to effectively recruit, what do you think your career will look like in five years? Now, what do you think the next five years will look like if you could recruit the exact type of sales team you've been dreaming of?

______________________________________________

______________________________________________

______________________________________________

On a scale from 1-10, how committed are you to reaching your goals? If you didn't say 10, what would it take for you to get there? Whatever that is, DO IT!

______________________________________________

______________________________________________

______________________________________________

*"An organization's ability to learn, and translate that learning into action rapidly, is the ultimate competitive advantage."*

**Jack Welch**

salesrecruitingu.com

# Chapter 2

# Key Things To Know Before Building Your Dream Team

---

In mid-2018, I started working with a top-notch roofing contractor out of Missouri. At the time they had seven sales reps and were looking to grow their team to 20+ reps in the Kansas City area. They knew that their goals were possible because other companies, just like theirs, were doing that, and more. They had all the right things in place to attract and to offer an incredible opportunity to top talent, but just like 95% of the sales organizations out there, finding top-notch people, without wasting a ton of time with the wrong people during the process, was just really tough for them.

Most of their sales force had been with their company for years, which made sense to me because their compensation, benefits plan, sales program and sales leadership were all on point, so retention wasn't a major issue and they built loyalty through all of those things. This was unique, as most companies that have commission-based sales opportunities are lucky to retain even 40% of their sales force, year after year, so I was amazed to hear that this organization retained virtually 100% of their sales team for so long. However, they didn't have a proven system and process for recruiting new localized sales talent, and they were spinning their wheels trying to make it happen. They needed help.

After I explained our system and showed them how this system could be theirs and implemented within their organization in a matter of two weeks, they immediately invested into our program. Action takers! The type of people I love to work with. This is when the rubber hit the road. We created their ads for Facebook, LinkedIn, Indeed, ZipRecruiter and Instagram, virtually automating their screening process so they weren't wasting time with the wrong people. We created their group interview presentation and trained them on exactly how to close the rockstar recruits they got in front of.

Within just two weeks of launching their new recruiting program, the sales manager recruited and onboarded 11 new sales reps, and ultimately retained seven of them after thirty days. In short, they KILLED it! Of course, as most companies would be, they were a bit overwhelmed when onboarding 11 new sales reps in a two-week period, but bottom line they were able to achieve success quickly by plugging in the right systems and taking action. From there, things gelled, as they onboarded, trained and supported their new sales team. From there, they did all the right things by not slowing down, continuing to recruit and onboard sales talent like clockwork.

Sometimes I wish all of our clients had a great experience like this, but they don't for multiple reasons; poor leadership, poor onboarding, poor training and the list goes on. But this company did virtually everything right. After we got their sales team built to 20+ in Kansas City, they decided to scale-up in additional markets which was something they hadn't even planned on in the first place. SWEET!

They had an original goal, they committed to it, hit their goal, and finally understood what was possible from a recruiting standpoint. From there, they decided to take advantage of what was possible, and they scaled up their entire operation to ultimately accomplish new, bigger and even better goals. Exciting stuff, and they deserved it! By them growing and nurturing their dream sales team, this company was able to excel and predictably grow, and they did it quickly! And, guess what? This could be you. Yes, that's right. The exact same thing can happen for you; the entrepreneur, the business owner and the sales leader thinking big about their future.

I want you to understand that accomplishing what you have not accomplished before first begins with the right belief system. This really clicked for me when I heard Andy Frisella talking about it on his podcast, The MFCEO. He was saying that if you do not fully believe in yourself, and if you are not fully convinced that success is a part of your future, that you will never actually do what it takes to see the success you dream of every day.

In this case we're talking about recruiting, and if you're not fully convinced that you're capable of building your dream sales team, then you never will because you'll always quit before obtaining your goals. After hearing that from Andy I became self-aware to the fact that I've naturally thought like this since my early 20's. For example, when I got my second sales job at this incredible company called New American Funding at 22 years old, I knew that making 10-20 grand a month was possible, and I believed that I could do it because others around me were doing the same thing, and more.

When I hit my first big goal of making more than $10,000 in a month, it was awesome because of the money, but most importantly, it anchored my mindset to a six-figure type of income. What I mean by that is I knew there and then that I was never going back to making crap money. 10 grand a month or more was my new minimum. I then became even more confident in what was possible, and I realized that if I could make $10,000 plus in a month, that I was capable of making $20,000 plus in a month, and guess what? I did it in a matter of three months, and my goals have only gone up since then.

I remember running around the office with a check for just over 22 grand in my hand, thinking I was the coolest cat in the room. My point is, the same idea and thought process holds true for recruiting as well, just like with that roofing company in Missouri. They knew that building a rockstar sales team of 20+ was possible because of other contractors doing the same, and I knew that I could make more than $10,000 to $20,000 in a month selling mortgages because other reps were doing the same thing, and sometimes a lot more. Both the contractor and I started out with the right belief system, took action, followed through with a long-term mindset (Even though in these examples we hit our goals quickly) and executed.

The truth is, if you don't believe that your goals are actually possible, guess how likely you are to achieve them? You won't.

If you do believe you can achieve your goals, and if you are willing to develop the right systems and processes necessary to achieve them, then you can, and you will! Just make sure you're not selling yourself short. Make sure your goals are massive, and make sure that they challenge you to grow beyond where you are at right now. Goals that don't have the end result of changing your life in a massive way will not inspire you enough to take the massive action necessary to actually accomplish them. I love what Grant Cardone said, "The single biggest financial mistake I've made was not thinking big enough. There is no shortage of money on this planet, only a shortage of people thinking big enough."

But even when you have the right belief system in place, you need the proper expectations on what it will take to get there. Building a great sales organization takes time and money. Cash is king when it comes to building a top performing sales organization. And, the initial investment of time it takes to create systems that will eventually run themselves, well that is a huge investment as well. So, yes, you have to believe you can reach your goal - exceed your goal – but you also have to be realistic and deliberate in how you will get there.

What's critical to think about here is the 10/30/60 rule. Imagine recruiting 20 sales reps in the next two months. 10% (2 reps) of those reps will be your new top reps. 30% (6 reps) of them will be average reps that you see production from if you have a solid compensation plan and onboarding program followed up by solid leadership. The other 60% (12 reps), even if you have a good program in place, will just fall off and leave the organization within 1-4 weeks because they just aren't a fit for sales, or your program (10/30/60 are average numbers and can fluctuate up or down depending on the quality of your sales program and opportunity).

The point is that you'll want to understand the numbers so your future growth goals align with your actions. The last thing you want is to need five reps, then only think you need to sign on five reps, later to find out that only one, maybe two of them are sticking and producing over time, putting you back into a mode where you're scrambling to get the additional recruits and sales production you need to hit your goals, when in the first place your goals should have been to recruit around 20-30 reps, with the intentions and expectation to retaining 5+ solid ones.

See, when your expectations are on point with reality, and when that 60% (Or whatever the numbers are in your scenario) starts to drop off, it doesn't drive you crazy because you're expecting that to happen already. You know that it's just part of the game. You understand beforehand that you need to recruit way more people then you actually need, to build that dream sales team you desire. The end result is you're not losing your mind because you're worried about retaining reps, that for one reason or another, just are not destined to stay in the organization. But instead you're calm, collected, letting them drop-off, as you continue to recruit, onboard, build and develop more new sales people.

When your belief systems are on point and you're confident about your future, and when your expectations are realistic, there will be a time that comes where you finally hit your goals, but you cannot stop recruiting at this point. Think A.B.R. - Always Be Recruiting! Don't wait until your sales forces loses its superstar to fire up your recruiting program again; consider successful sports franchises that make billions of dollars every single year. Even they anticipate their superstars dropping off, leaving, retiring or getting hurt, so they build a "deep bench" of future recruits. They aren't thinking, "We don't have to worry about talent right now because we're in the top 10." No, they think, "How do we find even more talent so that we can maintain this success and become even better over time." This same concept applies to building a sales organization.

Time and time again, I see organizations claim that they recently had a "good round of recruits come on board," which from my experience means that they just hired a few reps (Like within the last few days), and that they are happy with where they're at right there and then. Little do they know that things are about to change. This kind of thinking, "recruiting is going well right now," is typically followed up by organizations letting off the recruiting gas pedal, and things turning out in a way that they weren't expecting; reps start dropping like flies. For some reason they muster up some certainty that these new recruits are going to be "the ones to really help scale up this company." But the truth is that no one knows that for sure, and more times than not those reps do not succeed (Remember the 10/30/60 rule? Yes it's a number game as well...), and the organization virtually repeats the same cycle over and over again; they sign up a handful of reps, a percentage of those reps don't even show up for training, and the rest barely stick it out a week or two, with maybe one putting in a deal or two before falling off. It's a constant start-stop type of recruiting cycle that is random, not predictable, and it definitely doesn't align with what the top 5% of sales organizations on this planet do to grow their sales teams. Don't fall into this trap of constant start-stop recruiting cycles! Remember A.B.R., Always Be Recruiting, even when the day comes that you think you've arrived at your "Dream Sales Team."

## Hohman's Homework

---

What would you say is your average retention rate for successful sales reps? Be conservative and assume that a successful sales rep is one who brings in the expected average monthly sales production/revenue.

________________________________________

________________________________________

________________________________________

Understanding your average retention rate along with your sales production/revenue goals, how many reps do you actually have to recruit considering the 10/30/60 rule?

________________________________________

________________________________________

________________________________________

Do you believe that you can reach your sales production/revenue goals, or is it just a pie in the sky type of idea? Why or why not? If not, what do you feel needs to change for you to have the right mindset going into this?

________________________________________

________________________________________

________________________________________

If you end up struggling throughout the recruiting and onboarding process to reach your sales production/revenue goals, what will you do about it? And why? Remember to have a GREAT reason for WHY you want to accomplish these goals, or you will never work hard enough to get there.

__________________________________________________

__________________________________________________

__________________________________________________

*"Successful people do what unsuccessful people are not willing to do. Don't wish it were easier; wish you were better."*

**Jim Rohn**

# Chapter 3

# Quality Onboarding Is Foundational To Your Success

---

I can't tell you how important quality onboarding is to successful sales recruiting, and ultimately a successful sales-based business. Without a quality experience, your sales recruiting will never get ahead of the game, and you'll always be playing catch-up. Likewise, without ongoing support and love from the executive leadership team, your sales staff will always be looking elsewhere for a better opportunity, especially your superstars.

Sales is a tough gig. You have to be able to put up and brush off rejection, every day. You have to be able and willing to work long hours, sometimes. The rewards can be immense, but to support the right types of reps who are willing to do the work, rejection, and typical difficulties that come along with a sales role, a great onboarding and support experience are critical.

Half of the time when we take on a new recruiting client, we have to restructure their onboarding program so that reps are being taken care of properly. The structure depends on what kind of human and financial resources a company has. Some of my more successful clients already have this dialed in; with solid mindset, product, service and sales training, along with leaders training new recruits on the phones or in the field, spending more than enough time with new reps to ensure that they see success.

In these organizations, everything about the onboarding process is organized and scheduled; from group interviews, to final interviews, payroll processing and training, and from regular communication and support, as well as effective tools.

Of course, not every sales rep retains. But, if you have a great onboarding and training system, then there are no excuses for the recruit to fail. Basically, if the rep doesn't see success, it is because they couldn't get through rejection, couldn't close like they claimed they could during the interview (We've all seen that one happen), or didn't want to work hard enough to see the success that they claimed to want for themselves. You have to give your new reps every opportunity to see success quickly, and that's what a good recruiting and onboarding experience provides.

One of my best clients, a solar company, had his system dialed in. In the first week we were helping him with recruitment, he brought on a meat clerk from a grocery store, a tobacco salesman, a wine salesman and an ex-professional athlete. They all started on the same day. One of the new reps fell off within two weeks, and the others went on to sell 21 jobs within four weeks of completing their training. That's hundreds of thousands of dollars in sales from one month of effective recruiting and onboarding.

Now, these results are not necessarily typical, but certainly possible, and I bring them up here to show you the potential with a great program. Unfortunately, this piece gets overlooked more often than not. Owners and sales managers, as well as entrepreneurs, think that most people they hire are going to be just like them (Top 10-percenters) - I know you remember the 10/30/60 rule by now, right? Well most of your reps are not going to be in that top 10%, so don't assume that every recruit is going to "kill it as long as they work hard." That's just not how this works.

See, top 10-percenters can walk into just about any opportunity, know virtually nothing about the product, grab the sales script, do their own studying, and within a week or two be one of the top reps at that company. But most people aren't like that, and need a lot of training and leadership support to see even average success. The best recruiting program in the world won't overcome a crappy onboarding, training and support system for your sales reps

Not to drive this point to death, but did you know that companies with solid onboarding and training programs retain on average over 80% more of their new recruits, and have an average of over 70% more in production from their new recruits compared to their competition who just throws their new reps to the wolves? It makes sense why, right? It's clear. They invest time and resources into their people.

Let's go through some of the core things you should be implementing immediately in your onboarding process:

## **Setting Proper Expectations**

Starting from the beginning of the recruitment process, make sure your reps know what to expect; the good, the bad and the ugly. Don't overpromise and be honest about what they can expect to achieve. Have them commit to those expectations up front so that you can hold them accountable. Let go of reps who are not fulfilling on their commitment. Remember that YOU'RE the one with the opportunity.

**Organized Onboarding and Training**

Think of the first 30-days of your reps' work as a continuation of the recruiting process. Make sure everything is organized for them, and that you know your stuff, inside and out. Make sure your onboarding process is structured, "on paper," BEFORE bringing on new reps. That way both you and your new reps can stick to the plan. DO NOT wing it with this stuff or new reps will look at you as unprofessional.

Online training, in-class training, and in the field or phone training should be comprehensive and supportive. Leave no "excuses" for sales reps to fail. Make sure to train your sales reps on the sales scripts, top objections and responses, common product or service questions, and specifications and details about the product or service that may be important in the selling process. Again, have all this organized, along with any technology and tools they need, and make sure that it's all easily accessible for them.

This piece also includes making sure that payroll is all set to go when it's time to pay that sales rep for the first time. If you're late in paying your reps, or if their check is messed up, it brings in a lot of doubt, and the last thing you want to do with a new commission-based sales rep is give them any immediate reason to bail on you. The reason people go into sales is to make, potentially, a lot of money; make sure they are getting their cash quickly. They want to feel supported, and they want to be rewarded for their work, especially if they deserve it.

If I had it my way, every single one of my clients that runs a field sales organization, sometimes even some of our call-center clients that set their own appointments, would adopt a setter-closer model. This is where someone sets the appointment (more entry level), and another person closes the appointment (more senior level). These models tend to have the greatest success because new hires are pushed into the entry level part of the job first, which is great when you have a sales program that can bring in non-industry experienced professionals.

Another great thing about this is that the new recruit gets to see a progression within the organizations as they perform and bring in results. For example, a beginning sales person in the company can start out by setting appointments. If they do well, they move into the sales role where they are now closing the appointments they are setting, and if they kick butt from there, they can transition into the closer, more senior sales role, getting pre-set lead opportunities set by the entry level setters in the organization.

I love this process in a commission-based sales program because it gives new people an opportunity to see quicker money and success, which naturally results into better retention rates. It may not be the model for you, but I hope it gets your wheels turning. Bottom line, the goal is to have the quickest and easiest path to success and income. If that means changing up your sales program a bit, then I would definitely consider it.

Finally, make sure your team has effective tools in place BEFORE they get into the field; larger companies might integrate with advanced technologies and CRM's like NetSuite or Salesforce. A great and affordable CRM program like Pipedrive can help your sales team track where they are with their customers, and can be a perfect fit for you if you are still running your program off excel. The top field sales organizations in the world also use programs like SalesRabbit, which helps track sales territories and activities, as well as leads and communication tools so management is simplified.

Speaking of...

## Consistent Communication

The key to initial and ongoing success of your sales staff is effective and consistent communication. Especially in the beginning of their work with you, meeting daily can be especially effective, say for the first week. After that, once a week in the first month, and maybe even pre-set micro meetings within that first month to do quick check-ins or morning huddles. Make yourself, or make sure your sales manager is making time to work with your new recruits to ensure they have everything they need to succeed. And don't waste time with new recruits who are not putting in the work. Only invest time into the top 10%, and the following 30% who have the potential to do well in your organization. Remember that 60% or so are naturally going to fall off so just be OK with that (The 10/30/60 Rule).

## Positive Company Culture

I can always tell when my clients are doing things right by the emails and texts I get from their new recruits. I hear things like, "Thank you so much for setting up my interview... this company is awesome; great training, great culture and the people are incredible. I'm super happy." Doesn't that just say it all? Great training, great culture and great people… Sounds simple, right? Not really. Unfortunately, this isn't always the case and end result for a lot of companies; they may be good at persuading people into onboarding but if their sales program sucks or if they don't provide a great experience and culture, their program will continue to create weak sales production results, and reps will drop like flies. Creating a positive culture takes massive effort, planning, implementation and execution to see results.

A positive feeling creates a feeling with your sales staff; it's unspoken, but it's known. People feel good about the company, themselves, their colleagues. They have confidence in the company; that it's on the right path. There is also a feeling of things being interesting and fun. The best companies create a culture where virtually everyone on the team feels that they are involved in a really ground-breaking way. When there is a positive culture, people like their jobs!

A great culture puts wind in the sails of everyone at the organization. They trust the company, and the leadership. They know that if they work hard, and participate in a positive way, that they have advancement and growth opportunities waiting for them. When I think of a positive culture, I think about the leader first. Great leadership, great culture. Crappy leadership, crappy culture. Leadership drives the whole shebang.

Also, the most successful companies that I've worked with offer additional experiences to help their sales force develop all their natural gifts. For instance, they may take their top reps to seminars, maybe they'll have a book club around sales and leadership, or leadership training programs for reps that are stepping up within the company. You get the picture. What keeps people investing their time and energy into a company is if they see themselves growing and improving, with opportunities clearly mapped out for them and their future.

This culture should exhibit strong, ethical values, from the top, down. It should support and encourage high performance; anything less is unacceptable, which means you have to sometimes let people go because they're not living up to that expectation. A positive culture also means valuing and rewarding continued learning and development of skills and knowledge. This includes personal AND professional development opportunities. If you can provide a work environment where people feel that they have opportunities to advance their career and income, then you will retain the best sales reps out there. The best companies also nurture a culture of service, inside and outside of the company; encouraging helping others and giving back to the community-at-large.

## **Building Relationships**

As any good sales person knows, the best way to "make" a sale is to build and nurture a positive relationship with their client. The same holds true for your sales reps; think of them as a family, that will be providing your organization's revenue stream for years to come. Creating opportunities for them to build and nurture relationships within the organization is just as important as your relationship with them individually, and as a team. You basically want to create a sense of community, and that's born out of a positive culture of communication, learning and relationships.

## Effective Management and Leadership

A talented leader can transform your sales team. If it's not you in this role, make sure to have someone in this role who cares as much as you do about creating and implementing proven systems and processes around everything within the organization. Leadership and management are not about micro-managing or being overly critical. It is a true coaching philosophy; knowing your stuff, being organized, patient and persistent. Trust and empower your sales force to take ownership of new responsibilities, including helping with training.

When I worked as a mortgage sales rep, my sales manager, Mishel, invested his time and resources into helping me grow. He helped me develop professionally and taught me how to be a better salesperson, and ultimately helped me get to the point of making 10-20 grand plus per month. This opportunity changed my life, and his support and leadership helped me realize my potential; not just in sales, but in other areas of life as well. I literally would have taken a bullet for this guy. Everything hangs on the leader; and below him or her should reflect what that leader values because they've woven those values throughout the culture of the organization.

We'll be exploring how to develop sales leadership in the next chapter, so I won't get too detailed here. Just be tuned into this, always! If your sales leadership sucks, so will your sales team. Good leaders make average sales reps better. Great leaders inspire greatness in your team, and that will help with retention, revenues and overall success.

It's not surprise that the number one reason people leave their jobs is because of poor management.

## Hohman's Homework

---

Rate yourself, from 1 (terrible) to 10 (awesome) on the categories we discussed above. BE HONEST! If you are reading this book, chances are you need some improvements, so let's start wrapping our heads around things specific to onboarding and retention. Include any initial ideas on how you can improve in each of the categories below.

Setting Proper Expectations: What will do to improve this over the next 30, 60 and 90 days?

1 2 3 4 5 6 7 8 9 10

______________________________________________

______________________________________________

______________________________________________

Organized Onboarding and Training: What will do to improve this over the next 30, 60 and 90 days?

1 2 3 4 5 6 7 8 9 10

______________________________________________

______________________________________________

______________________________________________

<u>Consistent Communication</u>: What will do to improve this over the next 30, 60 and 90 days?

1 2 3 4 5 6 7 8 9 10

______________________________________________

______________________________________________

______________________________________________

<u>Positive Company Culture</u>: What will do to improve this over the next 30, 60 and 90 days?

1 2 3 4 5 6 7 8 9 10

______________________________________________

______________________________________________

______________________________________________

<u>Building Relationships</u>: What will do to improve this over the next 30, 60 and 90 days?

1 2 3 4 5 6 7 8 9 10

______________________________________________

______________________________________________

______________________________________________

<u>Effective Management and Leadership</u>: What will do to improve this over the next 30, 60 and 90 days?

1 2 3 4 5 6 7 8 9 10

______________________________________________

______________________________________________

______________________________________________

*"Culture eats strategy for breakfast, lunch and dinner."*

**Peter Drucker**

*salesrecruitingu.com*

# Chapter 4

# Sales Teams Will Either Rise Or Fall On Your Leadership

---

How many times have you seen in professional sports where an ex-superstar player takes on a leadership role, maybe a coach or a team manager position, and they fall flat on their face? See the truth is, most great players are not great managers or leaders; and yes, there are exceptions. But my point is, the same holds true for sales teams. If you're in dire need of leadership, don't jump to the conclusion that your lead rep is going to be the best fit for your leadership role because you feel that they can effectively show people how to do the job. Although that line of thinking makes sense, filling a leadership role in your sales team goes much further beyond just picking your top talent to lead the team. The reason this often fails is because the character traits that make a great salesman do not necessarily make a great sales leader.

Let's do a quick comparison....

According to the Harvard Business Review, the Seven Personality Traits of Top Salespeople are:

1) Modesty. This one surprises people, but instead of establishing themselves as the focal point of the sale, top salespeople position the team as key to helping them win the account.
2) Conscientiousness: Top sales people have a strong sense of duty, loyalty and are responsible and reliable.
3) Achievement Oriented: These are people who are fixated on achieving goals and continually comparing current performance to potential.
4) Curiosity: Your best sales reps have an intense hunger for knowledge.
5) Lack of Gregariousness: Another shocker for most of us to see, but it makes sense when you pick it apart. Overly friendly sales people can't establish dominance, which is crucial to clients taking their advice and recommendations.

6) Lack of Discouragement: There's an interesting link here that most successful salespeople played sports in high school; they're OK with losing a lot to get to the ultimate goal, and can bounce back quickly.
7) Lack of Self-Consciousness: This is what gives top sales reps the courage to make cold-calls, be action-oriented and be less inhibited when making a sale.

Now, let's look at what makes a great sales leader, or any organizational leader. According to the Forbes Business Development Council, there are eight qualities necessary for great sales managers and leaders. They are:

1) Gravitas. This is a fancy word for credibility. Sales reps will listen to, and follow, a manager they respect and who respects them as well as their clients. On the other hand, reps will not follow a manager they don't like or respect. But, gravitas is much more than popularity. It's a type of strength that only comes from integrity.
2) Empathy. Sales managers are people managers. Empathy is critical to building relationships. Relationships are critical to success in sales, leadership roles, and life, in general.
3) The ability to forecast. Great leaders have their finger on the pulse of the organization and the industry, and can plan and predict accordingly. The ability to

forecast, not just numbers, but trends, patterns and other attributes of the business or industry assure long-term success.

4) Active listening skills. Being present and in the moment with people is the basis for establishing trust. Does the manager or sales leader REALLY listen to what's going on in the field, for example? Do they listen carefully to what their sales reps are saying when it comes to their primary role?
5) Emotional intelligence. Important for sales reps, but critical for sales leaders. Knowing when to motivate, reign in team members, be a confidant, or support team members is key to leadership success in any organization. Is the sales leader or manager a grown up, and do they act like one?
6) The ability to challenge and inspire growth. Most of us respect leaders who challenge us to grow, but don't set us up for failure, over leaders who let things slide.
7) Adaptability. Billy Martin, the baseball manager extraordinaire, said once that if he has 25 players, he is 25 different managers. A successful leader adapts their style for each individual on the team, when needed. This includes adapting to different personality styles, traits and motivations.
8) A great understanding of the team's core job. The best managers remember how tough it is to be a successful

sales person, and are willing to get their hands dirty with and for the team. They have not forgotten where they came from before they were put in the position of being a sales leader.

Now, take a look at the two lists. Of course, a great sales rep can benefit from having the traits of a great manager, but do you notice how there is not that much overlap between the different skill sets? The sales rep has a more micro, or close-up view of their role in the organization, where an effective leader has to be able to negotiate in the micro AND macro perspective - seeing the overall picture, as well as all the details.

If you need leadership now, find the person on your team who exhibits the character traits of successful sales leaders, and develop them to move into your leadership role over time. Make sure they have the right skills, but don't assume they'll automatically know what to do in the position. They will also need to have structure and expectations, and leadership and management that they can rely on when needed. Likewise, they need to provide that for their team while at the same avoiding micromanaging.

There are a handful of ways to effectively recruit quality sales leadership. One way is by growing up reps within your organization to take on that role as we briefly discussed earlier. For most companies that need sales leadership right now, which is a lot of you reading this book, this will be the quickest path to success for you; but it will involve someone stepping into that leadership role in the meantime. Most of the time it's an owner who has to fill the sales leadership role in the interim, and on top of that they will need to actively recruit and/or pick out their future rockstar sales leader to be developed in-house.

Another way to recruit leadership is to organically draw qualified talent into your organization by being known as an innovative workplace with dynamic leadership opportunities, along with having a great sales program and incredible incentives. But this takes time, money, and involves having a top-notch sales program and online brand. EVERYONE should work towards building something like this, where you organically attract top talent into your organization, but it does take time, money and attention to detail as you create a better sales program.

My third and favorite way to recruit sales leadership is to leverage things like targeted Facebook, Instagram and LinkedIn advertisements to show up in front of qualified sales leadership; most of the time advertising to people who are already in that industry. With the right marketing and targeting campaign followed up with a great opportunity to recruit into (the opportunity definitely needs to be better than where they are currently at), you can sometimes get the attention of a current six-figure leader from another company who knows exactly how to do the job, and quickly fill a leadership gap that you need so badly. Keep in mind that this does take money, and a very appealing leadership opportunity to recruit into, to be able to execute on this strategy.

You probably noticed that none of those options to recruit leadership sounded easy, and it's because recruiting and developing leadership is hard. It takes WORK. But, regardless of how you fill the role, it's important to connect with people who you see as potential sales leaders, so you can at least build a recruiting pipeline of qualified candidates.

You can cold contact people through social media, meet leaders at network events, and the list goes on, but make it a top priority. A quality sales leader can radically impact your organization in a positive way. Oh yeah, and use social media as a digital relationship builder, not as a recruiting tool. You do not always have to go right for the "close." It's what you're looking for next year, or the following year - keep the door open for people who you know would be great in your organization, and build solid relationships with them over time. You never know when they are going to be open to new opportunities; maybe their company messed up their check, or the owner promised something to them that after a year still hasn't been delivered on. Bottom line, you want to be the first person that comes to mind when they think of exploring new leadership opportunities.

Your successful sales leader will know everything about the sales aspect of your business, company values, and take a keen interest in developing personally and professionally to be the best sales leader they can be. In their role as sales leaders, they need to make sure that the company's vision and opportunity are aligned with the goals of the sales reps on the team, holding the team accountable and coaching them to reach those goals, ultimately driving and executing on the vision of the organization with a well-oiled sales machine.

Can leadership skills be taught if they don't exist in the person? Maybe. I think the core personality traits for effective leaders are either there or not. But, specific skills can certainly be developed and honed, as long as the individual has a positive attitude, is willing to learn, is self-aware, and is humble but confident. Regardless, if you commit to developing your people into something greater than they are today, and provide opportunities for them to use those new skill sets to up-level their career in your company, they will step up in ways that surprise you, over and over again.

## Hohman's Homework

---

If you're reading this book, you probably are a leader or manager. Do you have the below skills and attributes? Rate your alignment with the eight traits below and suggest improvements that you can make over time.

<u>Gravitas:</u> How can you improve in this area?

1 2 3 4 5 6 7 8 9 10

________________________________________

________________________________________

________________________________________

<u>Empathy</u>: How can you improve in this area?

1 2 3 4 5 6 7 8 9 10

________________________________________

________________________________________

________________________________________

<u>The Ability to Forecast</u>: How can you improve in this area?

1 2 3 4 5 6 7 8 9 10

___

___

___

<u>Active Listening Skills</u>: How can you improve in this area?

1 2 3 4 5 6 7 8 9 10

___

___

___

<u>Emotional Intelligence</u>: How can you improve in this area?

1 2 3 4 5 6 7 8 9 10

___

___

___

The Ability to Challenge and Inspire Growth: How can you improve in this area?

1 2 3 4 5 6 7 8 9 10

____________________________________________________

____________________________________________________

____________________________________________________

Adaptability: How can you improve in this area?

1 2 3 4 5 6 7 8 9 10

____________________________________________________

____________________________________________________

____________________________________________________

Understanding of Team's Core Job: How can you improve in this area?

1 2 3 4 5 6 7 8 9 10

____________________________________________________

____________________________________________________

____________________________________________________

*"Everything rises and falls on leadership."*

**John Maxwell**

*salesrecruitingu.com*

# Chapter 5

# Push Hundreds Of Candidate Leads Through Your Pipeline

---

From 2013 through 2016, posting sales job ads on Craigslist, at least for me, and for a lot of you, was a GOLDMINE; it still works great in a few areas, but nothing like it did years ago. You could post an ad for $20 and get twenty responses within a day. A dollar per lead?! I'll take that all day long, and man, how I wish it was still like that.

Getting plenty of quality candidates through the door was easy back then, and it still is easy, but it just costs more, and the platforms are different. Just like anything else in business, the market changes, and if you're not on top of those changes, eventually the market will make it painfully obvious to you. If you're still just using Craigslist to generate candidate leads, and not getting the results you want, or what you are used to, that's the market telling you to make a change. And quick.

I think I just got lucky. In the first 18 months of my recruiting experience, and as a new entrepreneur, we could get away with recruiting solely through Craigslist ads. It was great, and we never had any issues. I was doing OK with my company - not as well as I wanted, but making progress in my business model, pulling in an income that at least paid the bills.

During one of my cold-call days, I got a hold of the director of sales at a national solar sales company called Evolve. They operated in 8 states and had about 15 sales teams and managers. This is when solar was just starting to blow up. I remember going through Craigslist to find companies to cold-call and seeing more and more solar companies popping up every single week. So, it was an exciting time for me to sell my services, and that sales director loved what we were doing so he signed up right away. They were pumped to see how easily we helped them blow up their Orange County, CA sales team. From there, a ton of opportunity came around, just through this one company, in several California, Massachusetts and New York markets. It was awesome. Another national client, in a new and growing industry. Sweet!

The timing couldn't have been better. In a fairly short period of time after I started working with them, they got an offer to be purchased by a global manufacturing company for around 50 million dollars. They gave me a call to ask if I wanted to consider filling their new Director of Recruiting role based in Utah.

Now, at the time, they weren't recruiting corporately, and virtually everything they built was done organically by their executive team and local field sales managers. If you read the forward to this book by Zac Kerr from Sales Rabbit, Evolve was the company he was referring to. But they didn't have anyone dedicated to a full-time recruiting role. So, I lucked out, because they already knew what I could do, so I was the one who got the first call.

As a side note, the whole reason I got into entrepreneurship was to make around the same amount of money that I was making in mortgage sales, but on my own terms. That was about 10-20 grand per month. When I received this offer, I was making OK money, but not anywhere near where I wanted to be. So, clearly, I wasn't happy with that, and was still not capable, at the time, of making the kind of money I wanted on my own terms, so I agreed to head up to Utah to meet them.

They flew me out to interview with them. At the time, I thought it was so cool to be flown out to meet with a massive national direct sales company. I remember thinking, “This is my first big business trip! I’m moving up in the game, baby!” Ha ha, dork. It’s funny because now I’ll do just about anything to not have to jump on a plane, unless it’s for a great reason. Once I arrived, I was picked up and taken to my hotel where I kicked back for the night, giddy about this crazy opportunity that I might get the following day.

The next morning, I woke up super early, got ready, and went straight to their office. I was nervous as heck because nothing this big had ever happened to me before. I knew that I wanted the job before they even told me about it. I didn’t care what I had to do, or what the pay was. I just wanted the opportunity, so I could learn more about recruiting and continue down the path of dialing in a proven system for recruiting high volumes of quality sales reps.

I met with the CEO, Dan Larkin, and Zac, who was their President of Sales, at their corporate office in Utah County. Obviously, these guys were on a whole other level than I was, and that intimidated me as a young entrepreneur, someone who was very eager for bigger and better opportunities. Although I was nervous as heck, I knew I could scale up their recruiting program better than any other person on the planet could, and during my interview I outlined exactly how it could be done within all of their markets, in a fairly short period of time. They made up their mind in about 45 minutes after meeting me and offered me the job on the spot!

They offered me a salary, plus uncapped commissions. I was 25 years old at the time, had been working in sales for about four years, and recruiting for just about 18 months, and I still was selling my recruiting services of course. So, since twenty years old, I had only earned an income through commission pay, and I thought the base salary plus commission comp plan was the coolest thing ever! I honestly wanted the job so bad that I would have worked all commission, moved up to Utah and lived in my car if I had to! Ha ha, maybe not. Who knows. But they offered me their position as Director of Recruiting, and provided an awesome comp plan waiting for me to plug into. It was all more than I expected, and obviously a no-brainer decision to make the move. My decision was quick, simple, and ultimately came down to three things when I think back to that moment.

First, I wasn't making the kind of money I wanted to be making working for myself. Second, I didn't go to college, and I figured this would be the perfect opportunity to circumvent that by having something substantial on my resume that could create long-term income opportunities for myself. And, finally, I was young - and stupid - partying and still throwing money out the window in Orange County, CA; I felt like this opportunity was a way for me to get past all of that, learn a lot more about recruiting, onboarding, and what it really takes to build a national sales organization like these guys at Evolve did. I knew there was so much more to learn. It was the perfect opportunity, so I took it as an obvious sign from God and accepted the position. It was time for me to step up my game as a sales recruiter and entrepreneur!

It all happened quickly; I flew back to Orange County on a Saturday, called my clients and let them know I was shutting things down, sold as much of my stuff as I could, stuffed the rest into my Honda Accord, and drove out to Utah six days later on a Friday. Everyone was shocked that I was leaving so abruptly, they thought I was crazy. Haha, yes, I am crazy! Finally, an impulse decision that paid off. I'm kidding… No wait, it's the truth!

One of the best parts about this opportunity was that, since the acquisition, no one was setting a budget for me to run the recruiting department. For some reason they gave me, this crazy kid, what seemed like an uncapped credit card with my name on it, to use for job advertisements, and for pretty much whatever else I needed. At least that's what it seemed liked to me, so I went crazy. Probably not the most professional move to make, but nobody complained, everyone was happy with the recruiting results, and that's just how it went down. Dan and Zac are probably laughing right now; they were so busy with the acquisition that I was able to just do my thing, however I saw most fitting. I experimented with everything from; Indeed, ZipRecruiter, LinkedIn, Facebook to

CareerBuilder, and all the rest in between. Not all of them worked well for me (more on that, later), but I "tested" the recruiting ad market like crazy. Literally tens of thousands of dollars per month.

At the same time, I purchased all sorts of software programs and recruiting solutions to see what could help me blow up their 15 solar sales teams even more than they had done themselves. It was like a whole new world of recruiting ideas exploded for me, and I learned a TON. Having the ability to work internally within this massive solar company, I was able to test out new job ad platforms, referral and networking ideas, and so much more. It really upped my game, and I'm super grateful to this day for that opportunity.

After about a month of working with them, I remember thinking to myself, "Ryan, you made the right move. You're going to be able to test everything under the sun so you know exactly what works, and what doesn't." I was confident that I could get to know this recruiting world better than anyone on the freaking planet. I was going to be the expert; I just knew it.

After the acquisition was final and I got my "uncapped budget," we were able to recruit just over 200 sales reps in about three months. It was awesome, and all in all, it was paying off. I learned about the many avenues of recruiting, beyond Craigslist, which led to more and better recruiting leads. A lot of mistakes were made before, during and after that opportunity, but the good news is that you have the opportunity to learn from me, and hopefully you'll do things better than I did.

Here are some key points that I learned about filling up the recruiting pipeline with hundreds of candidate leads.

- First. Don't forget about A.B.R., Always be Recruiting. I am pounding this concept in your head because it's incredibly important. This A.B.R. concept first begins with an ongoing flow of candidate leads coming into your recruiting pipeline. Every. Single. Week. Without enough leads, you will not have enough candidates to work through to have the proper end-result you need of onboarded recruits.
- Second. Paid advertisements are your path to predictable growth in your recruiting and sales program; this can include social media ads, and many other ad platforms that I'll touch on in a bit. This is the best and easiest way to bring on additional reps and sales production, especially if you do not have a current sales team pumping referral recruits into your recruiting pipeline. Let me ask you a question. If you could invest $1,500 over the next 30 days and bring on 10 new sales reps, with the end result of just retaining one great rep and three average full-time reps, would you invest the money? I hope so. If you said no, then you probably should close this book and call it quits. I

would say there's a mindset problem that needs to fixed if that's the case, and that you need to go back to chapter two. If you said, "Yes, but I don't have the funds yet," then close this book, go make some extra cash, and immediately invest a portion of it into your recruiting program. Learning this information alone is not going to be enough; it takes money, and action. Cash is king when it comes to building your sales organization, and it's important that you know that it's going to take time and a financial investment to get to where you want to be.

- Third. Referral recruits are statistically the best recruits, and your current top sales reps are usually the ones to bring in referrals, because they are making money and are happy with the job. Create an incentivized referral program for your current reps, so that they can make even more money beyond just their personal sales, by bringing additional value to the organization. I like to give smaller bonuses upfront for referrals, then larger ones once the referral recruit puts in their first handful of deals. For example, $100 could go to the referrer once the referral recruit gets through training, then an additional $500 could go to the referrer once the referral recruit puts in their first five sales.
  Regardless of how you tee-up your referral program, make sure there is something, and make sure your

current team knows about it. Make it a weekly discussion, and even think about running recruiting competitions around your referral program. Know that if you do not have any successful reps now, or if your sales program isn't great, then you're probably not going to get referral recruits. If that's you, work on creating a better sales program, then scale up your recruiting efforts with paid ads. From there you can start working referrals from those new recruits that have come on board through paid advertisements.

- Four. Most of the rockstart recruits are in the follow-up. The truth is, you will not recruit every great rep that you get in front of, and you won't be able to recruit every great contact that you have in your network. But you should be collecting and following up with solid contacts monthly to build real long-term relationships with them. From a recruiting perspective, this may provide you with a future opportunity to work with top performers. Imagine having a pipeline of 20 people that you reach out to once per month, one person per day, Monday through Friday, people who are all great sales professionals, maybe even some that are currently in your same industry. And now imagine that because you've been following up with them over time, and building a quality relationship with them, that you're the first person they think of when the time comes that they're looking for a new opportunity. You want to be at the top of a top performer's mind when they are looking for something new. That can easily happen with the right contacts and a consistent follow-up strategy. What if this type of strategy yielded just 2-3 rockstar recruits for you every year? At least for most sales managers, entrepreneurs and owners that I know, 2-3 rockstar recruits, per year, can make for a world of difference in the growth of their organization and their income.

Right now, I'm running my third sales recruiting company. The first two, I shut down because I was self-aware enough to understand that I didn't know enough about recruiting and running a successful business to make the "big bucks." In between running my recruiting companies, I worked at larger corporations that had sales offices all over the country, like the solar company I mentioned earlier. I learned more and more about the systems and processes of recruiting, onboarding, training and sales leadership.

Over the past five years now, I've served well over 150 sales organizations, and have spent over a million dollars on standard job ads, social media ads, referral programs and other tools to help companies build small to large scale sales teams, and those numbers continue to increase every single month. Of all my experiences, of knowing what works and what doesn't, I can unequivocally tell you that paid ads are the way to go when scaling up your recruiting program, especially when you do not have a massive network to recruit from. Let's take a closer look.

To grow a sales force, and I mean a sales FORCE, you will have to invest time in creating a great onboarding and retention/support model, but you will also have to spend money. Lots of it. Especially at the beginning, until you can start building an internal referral system of recruits. As I mentioned earlier, referral recruits statistically are the best recruits, so you do want to create a program that naturally produces those type of hires.

Referral recruits typically come from top reps, and are usually individuals who have similar values and are like-minded to the referrer, so they are typically a good fit for the organization. One of your top existing sales reps isn't going to push a crappy candidate into the organization, because they want to look good, and they want to work with like-minded people.

According to LinkedIn's Ultimate List of Hiring Stats, the number one way people find top performers is through referrals. In fact, two-thirds of referred employees refer at least one more person, so it's like a domino effect that saves money, too.

The biggest problem with referrals is that they make it tough to predict future growth, both from a human resource, and revenue perspective. For instance, if I want to grow a sales organization in Tampa FL, I cannot predictably say, "I'm going to get three good referral recruits in February, March and April, for sure. And that those new recruits will produce X, Y and Z." So, although referral recruits need to be a big focus for you, you'll still need to invest into the second-best way to bring on new, quality recruits, in a predictable way, which is done through paid advertising.

Unfortunately, for many companies, they've "tried" ads in the past, and haven't experienced what they consider success. But, typically, it's not the advertising that's "off," it's the whole framework and structure that is "off." They first have to remember the 10/30/60 rule, and understand that they will only retain, on average, 10-40% of their sales force. Secondly, they need to allocate appropriate funds for advertising, and place advertisements in the right places, with the right job titles and descriptions.

The typical cost per hire, we find, in today's market (2019) is around $150. For instance, as I write this, my company is servicing about 25 companies all over the country, and virtually every single one of them wants to bring on roughly 10 recruits per month, per market area. Because of the average cost per hire and their recruiting goals, they are investing around $1,500 per month to have the end result of around 10, fully onboarded recruits per month. Some of the better companies we work with have better sales opportunities and programs; they can recruit up to twice that amount with the same budget, or turn down their budget because of their cost per being lower.

As of today, I typically use four advertising platforms that I've found most effective, and allocate the recruiting ad budget like this:

1. Indeed (40% of the budget)
2. ZipRecruiter (25% of the budget)
3. Facebook/Instagram (20% of the budget)
4. LinkedIn (15% of the budget)

Just like sales, recruiting is a numbers game. I want the most bang for my buck, and platforms like the ones above bring in more leads per dollar. Now, this could change as different platforms emerge, and things change and shift, as they do year after year. But the point is that you need to invest. If the above formula doesn't work for you, it's not because paid advertisements don't work, it's because you need to adjust things to align with your company, industry and needs.

The above formula is just my standard one, a formula that typically results into home run results for our clients. If the above strategy doesn't work for our clients like we want it to, then we simply make adjustments, no big deal. Maybe the right formula for you is just using Indeed and ZipRecruiter; every industry and market area are slightly different, so tweak things until they are working for you. The goal in today's market should be to create candidate leads for $2.50 to max $5 per lead. If you can do that followed up by the right recruiting system and onboarding process, everything will work out in your favor.

Targeted social media ads can be a game changer as well. 90% of the time, the best potential sales reps are happy and successful in their current setting. So, they probably aren't making a career move anytime soon; but you can get their attention by going to where they are; Facebook, Instagram and LinkedIn. For example, right now, I can put a targeted ad in St. Louis that attracts people who are already in door-to-door sales by pointing out there are better opportunities out there for people like them; maybe lead opportunities, leadership opportunities, etc. It really depends on what you're looking for, and what unique opportunities you can provide within your organization.

Typically, 90% of successful reps are not searching on your standard job sites because, like I said, they are happy with their current setting. So, social media can be a backdoor way to reach and attract them into a recruiting system that they weren't expecting.

In general, I find, again in today's dollars, that if I spend $200-300 dollar on a Facebook ad, that it's very possible that I'll get one or two high quality recruits who will join the organization within a matter of 1-2 weeks (As a side note:

Your Facebook page should be tied to your Instagram account so that ads show up in both places, seamlessly, and in the same target market). If they are currently successful in the industry that I'm recruiting into, or if they are in a similar type of sales or leadership role, then I know my retention with this recruit will be, most likely, much higher than the industry average.

To get your wheels turning, for Facebook ads, as an example, you can put five different ads (for testing purposes) together for your target audience; maybe your target audience are direct sales professionals who are males in between ages 25-35 years old. From there, you can then limit those ads to a specific area, or open it up to a region, state, or the whole country. From there, you can launch those five tests ads and see which one is getting the best candidate leads at the lowest cost. Then you can shut off the other four ads that aren't as effective and scale the best ad up to get higher volumes of candidate leads. These strategies used for Facebook and Instagram apply to other ad platforms like LinkedIn as well. They take time and money to figure out, but once you do figure them out, it's a total game changer for recruiting qualified people, and one of the coolest things about it is, virtually every single one of your competitors isn't using this proven strategy.

With all this said, when it comes to social media ads, there are some things we can't cover specifically in this book;

for example, how to create the right audience, the right ad copy for your opportunity, visuals and landing pages that will yield the best result for your needs. Those all come out of experimentation, and I spent over $40,000 in 2018 just trying to figure it out for myself, because I knew it was going to be the next big thing in recruiting lead generation. You will not have to spend 40 grand, but you will have to invest some funds and experiment with different ads, pictures and videos to see what works. Job ads like Indeed and ZipRecruiter are definitely easier to master, but if you can crack the code on targeted Facebook, Instagram and LinkedIn ads, and if you can follow that up with a solid opportunity to recruit into; it can change your business, forever.

I'll wrap up this chapter by saying that even when you master generating candidate leads through networking, internal referrals, standard job ads and targeted social media ads; if you have a poor online presence, those quality leads that you're generating will be a waste of your time, and money. 70% of the candidates who are looking into your opportunity, will look at your website, your employee and customer reviews, and sometimes even you if they want to dive deep, and those percentages continue to increase every single year. If your online presence is not up to par with what the marketplace expects, then it will ABSOLUTELY hurt your recruiting game. Your company needs to look great at face value, and below are some key ways to do that:

- Have a nice website for candidates to review.
- Have good online customer reviews (4-5 stars).
    - Facebook
    - Google
    - Yelp
    - Etc.
- Have good online employee reviews (4-5 stars).
    - Glassdoor
    - Indeed
    - Etc.
- Be active on the top social media platforms
    - Facebook
    - Instagram
    - LinkedIn

In short, you want candidates to be impressed when they find you online, not turned off. The ideal scenario would be candidates are even more excited about your opportunity after doing their research; trust me on this, because they will be looking. If you're online presence is lacking, fixing it should be at the top of your priority list.

## Hohman's Homework

---

What kind of incentive do you want to create to encourage internal reps to recruit their friends? How will you roll this out to your team? And how do you plan to communicate it on an ongoing basis?

________________________________________________

________________________________________________

________________________________________________

How many sales reps do you need to recruit per month? Consider the 10/30/60 rule and figure out your monthly advertising budget ($150 average ad cost per recruit). When do you plan to invest into things like Indeed etc?

________________________________________________

________________________________________________

________________________________________________

Are your website, social media pages, customer and employee reviews up-to-par with what we discussed in this chapter? Be honest. What do you need to improve?

________________________________________________

________________________________________________

________________________________________________

*"Paid advertisements done right, followed up with the right recruiting system and onboarding process, are your keys to predictable growth."*

**Ryan Hohman**

*salesrecruitingu.com*

# Chapter 6

# Scratch Those Phone Interviews And Do This Instead

Building a powerful sales force is definitely a numbers game, as I've mentioned before. For every one superstar, you have to screen through, at times, hundreds of applicants. But, there's an easy way to screen out the bad apples. A way that completely eliminates wasting time with the wrong people.

Moving to Utah, into the Director of Recruiting role, like I said, was king of intimidating. I think most of us can agree that taking on new risks and challenges in sales and entrepreneurship is good, and necessary. But, a lot of the time, it can be a little scary.

Even though I was confident in my abilities, which were obviously strong enough to get me that role, I also knew I was stepping into uncharted territory. For me, and for the company. Fortunately, I was surrounded by some very talented and successful sales professionals and entrepreneurs. The flip side of this was also knowing that I needed to step up my game in a massive way, or it would become apparent, in the near future, that I didn't belong or wasn't truly qualified for the position. I used those concerns, whether they were valid or not, to motivate me to keep learning and getting better at my craft, as quickly as possible. The right fears can drive you in a good direction, sometimes.

You might be surprised to learn that by the time I got this director position, I still had never conducted even one phone interview. EVER. Everything I did was online, and the results for our clients were still amazing. But, that's crazy, right? How the heck was I running a recruiting company and seeing that kind of recruiting success, without ever actually speaking to any candidates?

Well, as I mentioned before, when I first got started in recruiting, my only advertising was done via Craigslist. At the time, I would post one ad per client, each day at noon, so I'd be at the top of the page. I would post ads and candidates would go through a specific emailing process, and I'd schedule one-on-one interviews with the best candidates for my clients. Each client typically had 10-20 interviews per week, so there was still a lot of work to handle on their end.

Over time, I improved this process, and scaled it up into a low-cost recruiting service, working in 20-25 locations at a time, month after month. Some of the companies I worked with were as small as 1-10 people, and some as large as 1,000+ people. But the localized recruiting process was always the same.

I was running this operation all by myself. I was the entire company. So, you can imagine the time it took to post ads in 20+ locations across the country, for multiple companies, recruiting for different types of sales roles, with different managers, office locations, interview availability and so on. I mean, honestly, successfully recruiting and building one office (location, territory, market area, etc.) is hard enough. How the heck could I manage 20-25 locations all by myself?

The online process that I used to screen and schedule candidates was amazing, and that's why companies paid me to help them, but I knew I could improve it when moving to Utah to help Evolve. I also wanted to impress the heck out of their executive team, and local field sales managers. When I was recruiting in 20+ locations at a time, a typical workday was 14 hours, with about 4 hours each weekend day. It was a ton of administrative work, and it SUCKED. But, I knew that if I kept continuing to improve the process, that I could do things for this solar company that were completely game-changing.

When I moved up to Utah, I set up my recruiting process for their 15 field sales managers across eight states. Once I received my "uncapped budget," ads were fired up across multiple platforms, and it was time to rock! My goal was to continue to improve the process as soon as possible, and I figured jumping on the phone with candidates who weren't responding to my typical online system would be the best way to do that.

They also provided me with an assistant, so I wasn't buried in administrative work like I was when running my recruiting company. This allowed me to delegate all the online work, and I was able to work on improving our systems and processes every day.

My emailing process had always worked well, but unfortunately only 40% of candidates who we reached out to via email would respond, so although clients were previously happy, I always knew there were a ton of people who could've been reached but weren't. The end result was pushing even more candidates to one-on-one interviews with my previous clients.

Since I had an assistant at Evolve, there were no excuses for candidates falling through the cracks like this. I was going to do my best to reach as many of the applicants as possible. So, we piggy-backed on my email system, and created a texting process for candidates who didn't reply via email. We texted them a simple message with a link to my calendar to schedule a call. At the time, I was using something called timetrade.com, and over time have switched to calendly.com for interview scheduling automation. Any candidates who didn't respond to our initial email would get this text and calendar link, and it started working! The text messages were getting high responses, and that link made it easy for candidates to pick a time that was convenient for them.

And check this out, my assistant managed all the messaging for me! Every day, like clockwork, I'd walk into the office with 10-15 phone interviews on my calendar, all scheduled automatically, sending candidates reminders to ensure they didn't forget about our phone interview. My show-up rates were incredible!

I've mentioned it before - sales recruiting is a numbers game. On top of hundreds of interviews being scheduled via email every week for 15 managers all over the country, I was knocking down 50-75 phone interviews per week, and working my tail off. I was closing down incredible people into 1099 door-to-door sales opportunities over the phone, and setting up managers with solid candidates who knew exactly what the job was about, and how difficult it would be to see success in it. They were high quality, pre-set interviews.

We increased our interview numbers by 15%, which was exciting to see. After three months and about 750 phone interviews later, I also figured out the perfect sales recruiter phone interview script, a literal step-by-step science to closing down candidates over the phone. I could talk a 65K salary plus commission, sales person, an engineer making 80K per year; pretty much anyone into knocking doors and working on 1099 all commission. It was freaking amazing! But unfortunately, at the three-month mark of running 10-15 phone interviews per day, I hit a wall. HARD.

Basically, my throat gave out on me. With all the energy and commitment that I had when explaining the opportunity to potential reps, every day, I was maxing out my energy on the phones, trying to get more quality people through the door for local field sales managers. They thought I was a machine. But with 4-5 hours of interview talk time, every day, and hundreds of phone interviews over a three month period, my throat couldn't take it. I had damaged it from talking so much, and by using so much energy over the phones, and it's still damaged to this day. But it was all worth it.

The good news was, our recruiting numbers were above target, and I was able to kick back for a month and see if I could figure out another way to push that additional 15% of candidates through the doors to our managers. Luckily, I had my assistant to run our typical emailing process which served up plenty of recruits for them. Since I couldn't do phone interviews anymore, I figured that if I could create texting templates, similar to our emailing templates, maybe candidates would choose an interview time that way, too. And it worked! YES! We would hit them with an email first, then with a 24-hour follow-up text message if they hadn't responded.

This increased our responses by 15% which is exactly what my phone interviews produced, but it was 10 times easier. AMAZING! I remember thinking, "Why the heck did I just ruin my throat over the past three months, when I could've been doing this instead." You live and you learn, I guess. The texting process was just as simple as the emailing process to manage, and after I created a system for it, that was delegated to my assistant as well. Sweet! I remember thinking, "Being a director is pretty freaking awesome!" It was so nice not to have to do everything by myself, like when running my recruiting company.

My goal was to get executive leadership, and every single one of our sales managers, to think I was the bee's knees of recruiting, so I was pushing them volume. But too much volume. They loved the types of candidates they were seeing, and the number of candidates we were sending, but they were interviewing too many reps, and couldn't keep up with their personal production and typical sales management responsibilities. Local field sales managers were conducting 10-20 interviews a week, while trying to keep up their own sales numbers, training 2-4 new reps each week, and trying to lead and manager their team.

Some of the managers were OK with recruiting volume because they had co-managers, but for most of them, it was madness, as you can imagine, doing everything on their own. So, even though it wasn't a bad problem to have, it still was a problem, so we had to figure out a solution, all while keeping up the momentum, as we scaled Evolves national sales force.

We discussed it with our top managers and executive team, and two of the managers brought up the idea of conducting group interviews to save time, while at the same time having the opportunity to still get 10-20 candidates through the door each week. A few hours of group interviews each week versus 10-20, one-on-one, 30-60 minute interviews? Brilliant! Wish I had thought of it first.

We organized the recruiting process to align for group interviews, launched it within two weeks, and quickly realized that it was a total game changer for our internal systems. Although not all the managers were great at the group interview piece, mostly because it was all very new, and I hadn't developed the process for it yet, company-wide results were still amazing. From an efficiency standpoint, everyone was super happy.

The bottom-line was happy, too. Our cost-per-hire decreased by over $100, which was significant when you multiplied that across 15 sales teams. We found that 40% of our candidates responded to the first email, 15% to the text, and another 10% by me picking up the phone to do quick option close on the group interview times we had available in whatever market the candidate was in. Things were running great, and the results were what we needed and more. I was starting to get good at this whole recruiting thing.

Your recruiting process, and the efficiency of that process, is critical to saving energy, time, and getting the most out of each candidate lead. The more efficient you become, the more you'll be able to do with your time and money, and it will be at that time, that you can have your cake and eat it, too.

Here are some tips to building an efficient and effective recruiting screening system:

- Know who you need before you waste time with anyone. What kind of sales personality, experience, and qualifications do they really NEED? Don't waste time with people that you wouldn't hire anyways, start with the end in mind. For example, if your sales reps need a car and a smartphone to be effective at their job, screen for basics like that first. You don't want to have an intentional discussion with someone who doesn't even fit the bid, right? Of course. So, don't waste time with the wrong people.
- Use technology to your advantage. Automate as much as possible. Save excessive back-and-forth time that you're probably experiencing right now, trying to get

them on the phone or in front of you. Emails and texts are perfect for this.

- Phone interviews are great, but they're not necessary to get the recruiting results you desire. Think about doing group interviews in your office, or via zoom. If you recruit high volumes of commission-based sales reps, then transitioning to group interviews is an absolute need for you. Group interviews eliminate the problem of no-shows, are a quick and easy way to screen out people who are not a good fit, and they are so much more efficient.
- Whether you're conducting a phone or group interview screening, make sure that your final interview happens quickly. This is a sales process, just like any other sales transaction. You have to close the deal quickly, and recruit and hire fast.
- Likewise, if someone isn't working out, let them go immediately - don't waste your time or energy. It's either going to work, or it's not. They're either producing or they're not. The moment it's clear that it won't work, let that person go. And don't worry, once you have a great recruiting system in place, you won't lose sales momentum. In fact, you'll gain momentum by getting the weak recruits out of your way. Out of site, out of mind.

## Hohman's Homework

---

What is your current screening and interview scheduling process like now? How would you like to improve it considering what you've learned?

____________________________________________

____________________________________________

____________________________________________

Write out three efficiency improvements you'd like to make to your overall recruiting process in the next 30 days? For example: "I would like to switch from phone interviews to group interviews, and I will do them via zoom."

1.

2.

3.

*"Efficiency is doing better what is already being done."*

**Peter Drucker**

*salesrecruitingu.com*

# Chapter 7

# Close Down The Top Sales Talent You Get In Front Of

---

I didn't mention it earlier, but I decided to move on from Evolve within a year. It's a long story of why, but in short, acquisitions are kind of a pain, and even though we had some incredible recruiting months, the company who acquired them was, well, let's just say, not doing their part. So, I decided that my next career move was going to be taking what I had learned from that experience to start my recruiting service up again. I thought, "Maybe now I've learned enough to crush it financially as an entrepreneur who specializes in sales recruiting." Immediately, I started reaching out to my past customers to fire things up again.

While I was starting up my services again, a handful of sales organizations from Utah were reaching out to me to have me go meet them; it turned out that a few companies heard about what I was accomplishing at Evolve, and they were interested in bringing me on as their recruiter. One of these organizations was, and still is one of the top home security sales companies in the country. A colleague referred me to meet with the CEO, and I was just blown away by everything they had going on. They owned this massive building to themselves. It was all new construction, with gorgeous modern furniture, all glass walls, incredible designs, the best company swag, sales tech, and really, to me, it was just all perfect. I couldn't believe that they were interested in me becoming their lead recruiter. Their office, and everything about them, was an opportunity that I had always dreamt about having.

Although I felt pretty set in my decision to start my company up again, I still met them. Quickly into our discussion, they offered me a $65,000 salary plus a commission opportunity. Now, this was a great offer, and it was 20K higher than I was making before. But, I told them that as sweet as their offer was, I really was more interested in taking what I had learned to ramp up my recruiting services again. I told them that one of my dreams was to be a successful entrepreneur that wasn't locked down to a corporate job. I offered for them to become a client of mine, and I would run the same recruiting program for them, regardless if I was providing a service or working internally with their company.

Well, they weren't interested in that. They wanted me exclusively "in house," and within minutes of saying "no" to their offer, they offered me a $100,000 salary plus uncapped, five-year, residual commissions on the alarm contracts that were sold - and full benefits. Wait! What?! Me?! A high school graduate who had to go to summer school twice, got terrible grades, dropped out of college, and partied like an idiot for half of his life? These guys were not messing around! This was an absolutely amazing offer, from an amazing sales company that had everything I would ever want in a recruiting role. When they gave me that offer, I remember thinking right at that moment, that I had built up enough skill sets in recruiting to become an official, **Six Figure Sales Recruiter**. This was something I had been working on for well over two years now. It was an incredible moment for me, and a sign that I was definitely heading in the right direction. But at this time in my career, I finally had learned to go with my gut. I was still convinced that I knew nearly nothing close to what I needed, to be "the expert" in my field, and that I needed to be in a really challenging position to get there.

I thought about it long and hard, and made the gut-wrenching decision to turn down the offer. This was, by far, the toughest decision I had made in my career up to that point, but I look back at it as a great thing, because it challenged me to not get comfortable at some monotonous corporate job that paid the bills. It was at this moment during my career that I started to build confidence in what I was pursuing, and it gave me the energy to continue pushing forward as an entrepreneur. I moved forward with ramping up my recruiting service again.

When I shut down my recruiting service previously, I had explained to my clients what had happened; that I had been offered an amazing opportunity in Utah, and that I just had to go for it. They were all bummed, but super supportive and understood my decision. So, when I called them back, about a year later, to fire things up again, they were happy to hear from me because they were still in need of recruiting help, just like 95% of the sales organizations in the world.

They were also excited about my new knowledge and experience around different job ad platforms and the concept of running group interviews, instead of 10-20 one-on-one interviews every week. It all made sense to them, and they were more than happy to sign-up for my services again.

A few months down the road, a lot my clients were complaining about the group interview process. Some of the candidates were walking out of the room during their pitch, and others weren't biting on the opportunity being offered. Unfortunately, at the time, I had no idea how to fix this. Most of my clients felt like the one-on-one interviews, although a lot more time consuming, gave them a better chance at pitching the opportunity and closing down the candidates they had. So, most of them went back to the old way I used to serve them; stacking up 2, 3 or 5 interviews every day, Monday through Friday.

Now, I knew this wasn't the right way to go because I had seen some massive success with groups interview at Evolve, and it was definitely more time efficient. But I didn't have the confidence, and or the process around group interviews to confidently tell them, "No, we are sticking with groups because of X Y and Z, and it will be a game changer for you. Here's exactly how you do it."

The mistake that I made at Evolve was not creating a proven process for doing group presentations, therefore not being able to train owners, recruiters and sales managers on closing a group of candidates down. If I had done that, I would have been set, and could have provided training to the companies who were struggling, but I couldn't help. To them, "group interviews just didn't work," but I knew that wasn't true.

I knew from my experience in working at the solar company, that managers who were good at the group interviews got the exact same recruiting results as when they conducted 10-20, one-on-one meetings each week. The only difference was that they did it in one third the amount of time, which literally took 10+ hours of recruiting time off their typical work week. But, since I didn't have that group interview process dialed in yet, I had to go with exactly what my clients wanted. I just wanted to keep them happy. Apparently, I still had more to learn. I remember thinking, "Why is running a company so freaking difficult!"

I started having doubts about my abilities to effectively build a company based on low-cost, recruiting solutions, and figured maybe the corporate environment was what I was destined for. After about 10 months of running the recruiting company, and realizing that I wasn't fit to be a six-figure entrepreneur yet, I reached out to that top home security company and asked if we could continue the conversation about my working for them as their lead recruiter. Crickets. I heard nothing. They were not responding to me, and I felt like such an idiot for turning down that 100K salary plus commission comp plan, with one of the best sales organizations in the country. This was a very stressful and low time in my entrepreneurial career.

Fortunately for me, and I think ultimately my clients today, I had built up a good enough network to land another great opportunity in 2017 working for Dan Larkin, again. He was and still is running two incredible companies, Encor Solar and Solo, which is a direct-to-consumer sales and fulfillment solution for companies all over the country.

I connected with them and made the tough decision to shut down my recruiting business again, since it was obvious that I still had a lot to learn. I still was wrapped up in providing low cost recruiting services for companies all over the country. But, I was still not making the money I wanted, and there were pieces that I was missing to be able to fully serve them at a high level. It was at this time, I felt like giving up on entrepreneurship and on trying to do this recruiting business on my own. So, I looked at several opportunities in Utah, and ultimately went to work with Dan and his team again, because the opportunity was amazing, I trusted them, and I had a previous relationship with them that consisted only of great experiences.

My colleague and friend, Ryan Roche, who is Encors and Solos President of Sales, was a blast to work with, and taught me so much about recruiting and the psychology behind it. He previously was the VP of Sales for a national home security company based in Utah. For years, he had been flying around the country, training sales leaders, conducting group interviews, and recruiting tons of reps under his regional and local sales management teams. He had been growing massive, direct sales teams like this, for 10 plus years, before going to Enro, and is known for being one of the best recruiters and top direct sales leaders in the door-to-door sales mecca, Utah.

Unlike my previous corporate job, although my core focus was still in recruiting, in this role I also had the responsibility of sales leadership. Ryan wanted me to fly around the country with him to ramp up and close down these massive group interviews that we set up. I got to see him do his thing, and it was freaking AMAZING! He was closing down reps who were six-figure earners at other companies, and converting them into 1099, door-to-door, sales reps, in a matter of 30-60 minutes. It was a blast to watch him close down 75% or more of the groups that we got in front of - every single time.

He would talk to the group about how Dan Larkin created Evolve, and how it grew to the point of selling to a global company, and how they had similar plans for the future for Encor and Solo. He talked about the culture, the growth opportunity within the company, and so much more. I quickly realized that people were drawn to the exact same things that I had mastered saying over the phones at Evolve. DUH! It was another, “How did I not think of this before!?” Thankfully, Ryan was there to make things click, and to help me master the process.

There was just one issue, at least in my eyes; he was still the one flying all over the country to do these presentations for local field sales managers. I think it’s just because he loved it. He had been working his tail off for 10+ years, traveling across the country, and though he never said it, I assumed he didn’t exactly want to fly around the country for another five or ten years, doing all the recruiting for his managers across the country.

I also wanted, selfishly, to create a group interview process that was duplicatable, so that I would have a system for it. And so that he, and the rest of the executive team at Encor and Solo, would think that I was "the man." So, after watching Ryan run a ton of group interviews, I outlined a step-by-step process, wrote it out in script form, brought it to him, and we dialed it in together within a couple days.

With his help, we were able to create a whole system for sales managers to study, so that the process could be delegated to them. We created training around the group interview process, got management fired up about doing them, and launched it in multiple markets all at once. BOOM! 16 recruits in week one, across four offices in four states. Brandon, one of the managers in Texas, recruited seven reps in his first week. He studied the script for an entire day and killed it. Why? Because he replicated exactly what was already working, and he trusted the process.

The whole point of this book is to help you develop and adopt systems, processes and strategies so that you can reach and exceed your recruiting goals. I want you to trust the process like Brandon and so many of my successful clients do, week after week.

Bottom line, whether you're running phone, group or one-on-one interviews, there are some key points that you should know and understand, if you want to be effective.

- Remember that the recruiting cycle is just like a sales cycle. Make sure that you have the right framework to build up the value of your opportunity and organization, and the right framework to close down the best of the best candidates you get in front of, just like Roche has been doing for well over 10 years now.
- Candidates are drawn to your company for several reasons. The history of the ownership, history of the company, what the company has accomplished in the past, what the company culture is like, what the future holds for people who are with the organization today, and the growth opportunities that exist within the company. Make sure you cover every single one of these topics in your interviews.
- Don't over-pitch the income and role potential or attrition will be even worse than it is for you now. Don't make general statements that are misleading like "Someone like you should make 10 grand per month easy, if you just do the work." Sure, maybe this can happen, but if it's unlikely for majority of your sales reps, new recruits will feel lied to after they come on board.
- Likewise, don't over-pitch the training aspect of your opportunity. Don't promise more support than can truly be offered. Be realistic. Be truthful. Better to underwhelm than overwhelm.

- Align your "close" with what potential recruits want to experience in their life kikeand career. Again, recruiting is like a sales pitch, but for a sales position. You don't want to be pushy, you just want to help them see how you can solve a problem for them; just like you do in sales. You want to help them come to the conclusion that your opportunity is THE opportunity that will help them achieve what they truly want for their future. This tends to happen more during one-on-one interviews, but can happen in a group setting when done right. To understand what a candidate wants in a one-on-one setting, you can ask questions like:
    - "What are you looking for in a sales position? Why?"
    - "What are your future goals? Why?"
    - "What do you want to accomplish in the next 12 months? Why?"
    - "What do you feel has been missing from your previous opportunities? Why?"
- If possible, share a success story that aligns with your potential recruit. For example, "This isn't a typical timeline, but John, who was this position and was about the same age with similar experience… He came on board, worked a 50-hour work week and made 4K in his first 30 days, 7K in his second month, and has been cracking 10K plus, per month, since. You remind me of

him because of X, Y and Z, and I don't see why you wouldn't be able to do the same thing. What do you think?"

- Attributes like resiliency, drive, initiative, self-confidence, problem solving and the ability to respond positively to feedback are all important to succeeding in any sales position. Don't worry if you bring someone on who doesn't exhibit those traits, because the truth is, you won't even know until their putting in the work or not. Scientifically, only 10-20% of someone's characteristics show up in an interview, so your assumptions about them during an interview are typically wrong; that's just the reality. Remember to hire fast, and fire fast when reps are not producing minimum expectations. A.B.R., and don't forget the 10/30/60 rule.

Make sure to build value in your program as a whole, and connect the benefits of your sales program to the candidates personal needs and future goals. They need to be able to envision themselves accomplishing exactly what they want to accomplish in life, by being a part of your organization. When you can effectively do this with a high volume of candidates, you will be able to quickly build your dream sales team.

## Hohman's Homework

---

What is your company's story? When, how and why did it begin?

__________________________________________________________

__________________________________________________________

__________________________________________________________

How have you been involved in your company's story? How has it impacted your life?

__________________________________________________________

__________________________________________________________

__________________________________________________________

What has the company accomplished thus far? And what are the future plans for growth?

__________________________________________________________

__________________________________________________________

__________________________________________________________

What growth opportunities exist within the company? And why are these opportunities unique from the rest of the marketplace?

____________________________________________________

____________________________________________________

____________________________________________________

What is the company culture like at your organization? And what does that really mean for people who join?

____________________________________________________

____________________________________________________

____________________________________________________

Do you have a successful sales rep story that can be shared during your interviews? If yes, what is it? If no, focus on creating at least one great success story in the next three months.

____________________________________________________

____________________________________________________

____________________________________________________

*"No matter what you do, your job is to tell a story."*

**Gary Vaynerchuck**

# Chapter 8

# Continue To Learn, Evolve And Improve Over Time

---

Throughout this book, I've shared snippets about my journey as an entrepreneur. It involved learning, growing, screwing up, trying again, learning more, and failing again, over and over. To say it's been a crazy cycle would be an understatement. Ed Mylett talks about the first five years of becoming great at anything, and how those years are typically full of false-starts; ramping up, failing and learning, over and over again, until things eventually click and you get the momentum. That was exactly my experience in trying to figure out how to be a great recruiter and entrepreneur. And honestly, I don't consider myself even close yet. But it's the ones who can make it through those difficult times of personal development and organizational growth, who will ultimately succeed at a very high level.

Even though I have moments where I think I'm at the pinnacle of my profession, the truth is, I'm not even close; and I know that in another five or ten years, I'll be saying the same thing, because there are always so many improvements to be made, for all of us.

You must continually challenge yourself, be honest with yourself and make improvements where you need it. Just like I've said about your sales organization, if you're not growing, you're dying. Well that applies to you as an individual, too. This is something that makes me tick; that constant challenge of improving and learning.

There are people and organizations, in your industry and market, that have far better systems in place, and who are building their dream sales teams right now. It's not because they're smarter or more talented than you are. It's that they've invested more time and resources in creating streamlined systems and processes around the topics taught in this book. They run with these proven systems and processes every single day, improving them over time. And it's these aspects of their business that create specific results for them, not as individuals, but for their business processes. And you can have that same type of experience, too. It just takes a commitment to developing the systems and processes necessary to build, exactly what you want to build.

I've worked with hundreds of different companies, mostly in the United States, and I can tell you confidently that only 5% of them know what they're doing when it comes to recruiting, onboarding, training, leadership support, and building a great work environment. My guess is that you're reading this book because you desire to be in that top 5% of sales organizations.

Your own self-awareness and knowing what you DON'T know today, followed up by massive action, is ultimately what will get you there. Learn from your prior mistakes, and the mistakes of others. Cut down your learning curve by learning from others' failures, like some of the things I outlined in this book. But, more importantly, learn from what others are doing right. You don't have to reinvent the wheel here. What works now is in place for companies all over the world, and if they can figure it out, so can you!

Let's recap some of the core strategies we discussed in this book, so you can continue to build your bulletproof recruiting, onboarding and sales program that will allow you to accomplish exactly what you know you can.

### *A.B.R. Always Be Recruiting!*

I know I've mentioned this a lot, but it's absolutely critical to your success. Sales recruiting is not a one-off thing. You don't just hire a few sales reps, especially ones that are 1099 commission-based, and expect them all to finish their careers with you. The attrition rate in this field is high, typically 60-90% depending on how good your sales program is, so you ALWAYS have to be recruiting, and have systems in place to do so, in order to reach your goals.

### *Generate High Volumes of High Quality Leads*

As you already know, I'm sure, from personal experience, sales reps come and go. Some will stay with you a few weeks, a few months, or a few years. Sales reps are always looking for great opportunities, so as long as you're providing that, and supporting them well, they'll stay.

But the reality is that retention is naturally abysmal in the sales industry; a great sales organization may retain only 40% of its people for 6-18 months. So, it's critical that you create a recruiting system that attracts quality, and quantity. It really takes both to accomplish your goals. Never forget the 10/30/60 rule.

Referrals are great for building your sales force; we find that if a rockstar refers another individual, it's usually a good fit. But, a referral-only based recruiting strategy is not enough. As a sales manager, I can't predict with any accuracy that I will get 10 new sales reps this month, based on referrals. I can, though, predict, accurately, how many I can bring in via paid advertisements. So - invest.

### *Screening Out Bad Candidates*

Save yourself some time, energy and grief, and get rid of the typical, long, one-on-one, phone interview process, especially if you're recruiting 1099 sales reps. In the time it takes to conduct one 30-minute phone interview, I can screen 10, 15, 20 applicants, either in an office setting or a zoom-type meeting.

By pushing people right into a group setting, you can almost immediately see who will fit and who won't. You can present your opportunity to a dozen or more individuals, at the same time, and see who is highly interested. If you invite 15 to a group interview, and a few don't show up, no problem - you still have the others to meet with, and you haven't blocked off your calendar, needlessly.

From there, you can run short one-on-one interviews with the candidates who are highly interested, and who you think would be a good fit for your sales program. If they aren't a good fit, then be OK with turning them down. YOU'RE the one with an opportunity, and if you're actively recruiting in the way that I've gone over in this book, then you'll have way more candidates in the pipeline, and you shouldn't be worried about turning people down.

If you hire someone who very clearly is NOT a good fit, and you find out after the fact, let them go immediately. Most of the time, if someone is going to work out, you will know it right away. ESPECIALLY get rid of the people with bad attitudes, who don't care about their productivity, and who bring down the culture of your organization. Your other sales reps will respect you for that.

### *Closing Down Sales Talent and Effective Onboarding*

Your pitch during the group interview reflects the culture and opportunities within the sales organization. You are making a sale, and the potential recruit is your "sales prospect." Just like any good sales process, you have to control the discussion, build value, be honest, and promise only what you can deliver.

Is your opportunity better than the most opportunities in your same market-area and field? It should be! Does your sales program align with the needs and goals of your sales reps? It needs to! Does your pitch make it very clear to your candidates how they can participate in the growth of the company? It definitely should! Be transparent about what it will really take to get there. Honesty is key.

Once your sales reps sign on, are you staying organized? Do you have a plan and system IN PLACE? Are you setting your sales reps up for absolute success, including product, service, sales and objections training? Do they have the tools that they need for success? Maybe a company email account, sales tracking software, a sales script and a uniform? Every opportunity is a little different. Make sure they have everything that they need to see quick success during the onboarding process.

Remember, not everyone is a 10-percenter, where you just can hand them a binder of information, and they're good to go. Give your new reps the tools and support they need, so that if they fail, it's on them, and not you.

### *Retaining Your Sales Team and Developing Leaders*

You have to give your sales team a reason to stay and excel. Provide opportunities for them to use new skills to up level their career, and to feel good about themselves and their role within the company. Do they like going to work? Have you created a sense of community and camaraderie? Do you offer personal and professional development opportunities? Have you created a positive culture?

People are drawn to your opportunity because of the potential to make money, at least top producers are. But, they'll stay because they can make money AND enjoy the work, their colleagues, and the job, in general. They will stay because they trust and respect the leadership, and believe in the mission and future of the organization. They will stay because you are showing them, and giving them, what they need to succeed and grow personally, and professionally.

None of these key topics above can be overlooked - there are no shortcuts. You can't achieve greatness as an organization, and true scalability, unless you have all these things in place, coupled with a great brand and online presence.

What you want to achieve can be as simple as implementing the systems and processes that I've outlined in this book. Continue to stay positive. Stay focused. Stay driven. And know that this could be your best year, ever. It's GO TIME, baby! Let's get to work!

## Hohman's Homework

---

What are the top 5 takeaways you've had by reading this book? And what do you plan to do with this information?

1.

2.

3.

4.

5.

*"Your greatness is limited only by the investments you make in yourself."*

**Grant Cardone**

# Need additional help?

Join me for a free sales recruiting training at:

www.sixfiguresalesrecruiter.com/register

YouTube: Ryan Hohman SRU

Facebook: RyanHohmanSRU

Instagram: ryanhohman_sru

LinkedIn: Ryan Hohman

Made in the USA
Middletown, DE
20 May 2019